WHIMS OF WISDOM

THE LIFE OF BAHLOL DANA

MOHD ASAD NAQVI

To the timeless wisdom found in laughter and the profound lessons hidden in simplicity.

To my family and friends, whose unwavering support and encouragement light up my journey.

To my grandfather and to all the seekers of truth and joy, may Bahlol Dana's stories inspire you to find wisdom in the most unexpected places.

Contents

TO WHOEVER READS,

Chapter 1

INTRODUCTION

In the Name of Allah, the Most Beneficent, the Most Merciful. All the praises and thanks be to Allah

In the annals of history, the name "Bahlol" stands out uniquely, not merely as a name but as a symbol of profound wisdom cloaked in apparent madness. While many might have borne this name, it is Bahlol Dana whose legacy transcended the ordinary, transforming the very essence of what it means to be a "fool." Through his eccentricity and keen intellect, Bahlol redefined the boundaries of wisdom and folly, leaving an indelible mark on the collective consciousness of his time and beyond.

Bahlol Dana was the only fool who knew what normal people did not, a man whom people actually called a fool yet could teach even the most knowledgeable individuals. His unique approach to wisdom made him a beloved figure, and the name Bahlol became synonymous with smiling, happy individuals who exude a sense of joy and contentment.

Born as Abu Wahab bin Amr in the city of Kufa, Bahlol was one of the wealthy inhabitants of Baghdad. Despite his affluence, he chose a life that seemed to defy societal norms. His eccentric behavior and apparent madness were, in fact, a deliberate facade, allowing him to convey profound truths and challenge the hypocrisies of his time. He used his perceived insanity as a tool to critique the powerful, including his own relative, the Caliph Harun al-Rashid. Some texts even suggest that Bahlol and Harun al-Rashid were cousins on their mothers' side, highlighting the close yet complex relationship between them.

Bahlol's stories have been passed down through generations, shared among families with excitement and happiness. These tales, rich with humor and wisdom, have captivated audiences for centuries, offering lessons that transcend time and culture. They reveal a man who, despite being labeled a fool, possessed an unparalleled understanding of human nature and the world around him.

A particularly significant aspect of Bahlol's life was his relationship with Imam Ali al-Ridha (Imam Reza), the eighth Shia Imam. It is said that Bahlol adopted his peculiar appearance and behavior as a means to support and protect Imam Reza, who was imprisoned by the Caliph Harun al-Rashid. The Imam's struggle was a painful phase in history, marked by fourteen years of imprisonment and suffering. The tragic end came with his death by poisoning, an act widely attributed to Harun al-Rashid.

Imam Reza's life in prison was fraught with hardship and persecution, a period that Bahlol witnessed with a heavy heart. His actions, often seen as mere folly, were in fact deeply rooted in a desire to shield the Imam and to subtly protest against the injustices inflicted upon him. Bahlol's apparent madness served as a guise under which he could navigate the treacherous political landscape, offering support to the oppressed without drawing the ire of the Caliph's regime.

This book seeks to explore the life and times of Bahlol Dana, delving into the rich anecdotes and parables that illustrate his unconventional path to wisdom. It aims to uncover the man behind the legend, to understand the historical and cultural context in which he lived, and to appreciate the enduring lessons he left for posterity.

As we journey through the pages of Bahlol's life, we will come to realize that his madness was, in fact, a profound method of teaching. He challenged the status quo, questioned societal norms, and in doing so, provided a new lens through which knowledge and ignorance, wisdom and folly, could be understood. In the end, Bahlol Dana did more than just change the meaning of a name; he altered the very perception of what it means to be wise. This book is based on historical information that was written during Bahlol Dana's time and has been passed down through generations Even today many of his stories are narrated in assemblies and teach the listeners valuable lessons.

In the following chapters, we will delve into the philosophical life of Abu Wahab, exploring the depths of his wisdom, his unique approach to teaching, and the timeless lessons he imparted. Through detailed examinations of his actions, interactions, and the stories passed down through generations, we will uncover the rich tapestry of Bahlol Dana's life and the enduring impact of his legacy.

Chapter 2

EARLY LIFE

Abu Wahab bin Amr, later known as Bahlol Dana, was born in the city of Kufa, a prominent center of learning and culture in the Islamic world. He lived during the Abbasid era, around the time of Caliph Harun al-Rashid (reigned 786-809 CE). From a young age, Abu Wahab exhibited signs of keen intelligence and a profound curiosity about the world around him. His early life in Kufa laid the foundation for the remarkable journey that would later transform him into one of history's most enigmatic and revered figures.

Family Background

Abu Wahab hailed from a well-respected and affluent family. His lineage was notable, and he was connected to influential circles within the region. This privileged background afforded him opportunities for education and intellectual development that were not available to many of his contemporaries. His family's wealth and status played a significant role in shaping his early experiences and perspectives. The lineage of Abu Wahab traced back to esteemed scholars and leaders within the Islamic community. His family's influence extended beyond Kufa, with connections to prominent figures in Baghdad and other major cities of the Islamic world. From an early age, Abu Wahab was surrounded by an atmosphere of intellectual curiosity and scholarly pursuits.

Education and Early Influences

Growing up in Kufa, Abu Wahab was exposed to a diverse array of intellectual traditions. The city was a melting pot of cultures and ideas, attracting scholars, philosophers, and theologians from across the Islamic world. This vibrant environment nurtured his intellectual growth and exposed him to the rich tapestry of human thought.

Abu Wahab's formal education included studies in theology, jurisprudence, and philosophy. He was particularly drawn to the teachings of the early Islamic scholars, whose works profoundly influenced his thinking. His mentors recognized his exceptional intellect and encouraged him to pursue a path of knowledge and wisdom.

Under the guidance of renowned scholars in Kufa, Abu Wahab received a comprehensive education honing his intellectual abilities and expanding his understanding of the world. Among his early influences were the works of classical Islamic philosophers such as Al-Farabi, Ibn Sina (Avicenna), and Al-Ghazali. Their writings stimulated Abu Wahab's intellect and instilled in him a deep appreciation for the pursuit of wisdom and truth. He absorbed their teachings with enthusiasm, eager to uncover the mysteries of existence and the nature of reality.

Signs of Wisdom

Even as a young man, Abu Wahab displayed an extraordinary ability to perceive truths that eluded others. His insights were often couched in humor and unconventional behavior, which both intrigued and perplexed those around him. He developed a reputation for being insightful beyond his years, and his peers often sought his counsel on matters of importance.

Decision to Adopt an Unconventional Path

Despite his comfortable life and promising future, Abu Wahab grew increasingly disillusioned with the materialism and hypocrisy he observed in society. He began to distance himself from the trappings of wealth and status, seeking instead a deeper understanding of life's true purpose. This inner conflict eventually led him to adopt the persona of Bahlol Dana, the "wise fool."

Bahlol's decision to embrace an eccentric and seemingly mad lifestyle was a calculated one. By presenting himself as a fool, he gained the freedom to speak truth to power and to challenge societal norms without facing immediate repercussions. His apparent madness served as a protective veil, allowing him to critique the powerful, including the Caliph Harun al-Rashid, without drawing the ire that such criticisms would typically provoke.

Chapter 3

BECOMING BAHLOL

The transformation from Abu Wahab to Bahlol Dana was not an overnight change but rather a gradual process influenced by his growing commitment to a higher moral and spiritual purpose. One of the most enduring tales about Bahlol centers on his strategic decision to feign madness, a choice that was deeply influenced by his devotion to Imam Musa al-Kadhim (a.s) (descendant of the Islamic prophet Muhammad and the seventh imam in Twelver Shia Islam). During the Abbasid Caliphate, particularly under the rule of Caliph Harun al-Rashid (reigned 786-809 CE), the political climate was fraught with tension. The Abbasid rulers were often hostile towards the followers of the Shia Imams, viewing them as a threat to their authority. Imam Musa al-Kadhim (a.s), the seventh Shia Imam, and his followers faced significant persecution. It was in this turbulent environment that Bahlol Dana's story unfolds.

According to a well-known tradition, a group of Imam Musa al-Kadhim (a.s)'s companions and close friends approached him for advice. They were aware that Caliph Harun al-Rashid was angered by their allegiance to the Imam and feared for their safety. The Imam, recognizing the danger they were in, offered them guidance in a single cryptic letter: "jim" (ج).

Each companion interpreted this letter in a way that resonated with their circumstances and understanding:

- **Jala Watan (جلاء وطن)** - Exile: One companion took "jim" to mean exile, deciding that fleeing the homeland was the best way to escape persecution.

- **Jabl (جبل)** - Mountain: Another understood it as a directive to seek refuge in the mountains, where they could find safety in isolation.

- **Jinoon (جنون)** - Insanity: Bahlol interpreted the letter as a call to feign insanity, a tactic that would allow him to evade the scrutiny and wrath of the Abbasid authorities.

Before embracing the guise of madness, Bahlol Dana was a man of considerable influence and power. He lived a life of majesty and splendor, respected and well-established in his social and possibly political circles. However, his unwavering devotion to Imam Musa al-Kadhim (a.s) and the Imam's cryptic advice prompted him to turn away from his former life.

By feigning insanity, Bahlol could navigate the dangerous political landscape without arousing suspicion. His behavior, seen as harmless and eccentric, allowed him to avoid persecution while still remaining close to his spiritual roots and the teachings of the Imam.

After deciding to feign madness, Bahlol drastically changed his way of life. He donned rags and chose the simplicity of desolate places over the opulence of Harun al-Rashid's palaces. His sustenance became a mere bite of stale bread, symbolizing his rejection of worldly luxuries and his dependence solely on God. He refused any favors or dependence on the Caliph or his courtiers, seeing their wealth and power as meaningless compared to the spiritual fulfillment he sought.

Bahlol's antics often baffled those who encountered him, but to the discerning few, his actions were laced with profound insights and lessons. He used humor and satire as tools to convey truths that were both timeless and relevant to the issues of his day. Through his unorthodox methods, Bahlol Dana became a revered figure whose wisdom was sought by people from all walks of life.

Through his apparent insanity, Bahlol was able to express profound truths and critique the injustices of the time without facing direct repercussions. His words and actions, though often veiled in humor and eccentricity, carried deep wisdom and moral lessons. This behavior not only protected him but also allowed him to remain a voice of truth in a time of widespread oppression.

Bahlol considered his way of life far superior to that of the Caliph and his courtiers. By rejecting material wealth and choosing a path of piety and humility, he demonstrated a profound internal freedom and spiritual superiority.

Bahlol Dana's story is a testament to his intelligence, strategic thinking, and deep spiritual commitment. His feigned madness was a means of survival, but also a powerful form of silent resistance against the corrupt and oppressive authorities of his time. His legacy continues to inspire, reminding us of the value of humility, wisdom, and unwavering faith in the face of adversity.

Chapter 4

THE PERSECUTION OF IMAM MUSA AL-KADHIM (a.s) & HIS FOLLOWERS

During the reign of Harun al-Rashid (786-809 CE), the Abbasid Caliphate was one of the most powerful and influential empires in the world. However, this period was also marked by significant internal strife and political turmoil. The Abbasid rulers were wary of any potential threats to their authority, especially from the descendants of the Prophet Muhammad, who commanded significant religious and moral influence among the people.

Imam Musa al-Kadhim (a.s), the seventh Shia Imam, was a key spiritual leader during this era. Born in 745 CE, he was known for his piety, knowledge, and deep compassion for his followers. As a descendant of the Prophet Muhammad, Imam Musa al-Kadhim (a.s) held a special place in the hearts of the Shia community. His leadership was seen as a continuation of the Prophet's teachings and a source of guidance in spiritual and worldly matters.

The Abbasids had originally rallied the support of the Shia community against the Umayyads by claiming descent from Muhammad's uncle Abbas. They promised to bring an Alid leader- one descended from Muhammad through his daughter Fatima and son-in-law Ali ibn Abi Talib—to power. However, when Abu al-Abbas al-Saffah (r. 750–754) declared himself the first Abbasid caliph, many Shias were disillusioned. They had hoped for an Alid leader, and the Abbasids soon turned against their former allies. This hostility intensified after the failed revolt of the Alid pretender Muhammad al-Nafs al-Zakiyya in 762–763.

Imam Musa al-Kadhim (a.s) was contemporary with the Abbasid caliphs al-Mansur, al-Hadi, al-Mahdi, and

Harun al-Rashid. Unlike his father, who often taught freely in Medina, Imam Musa al-Kadhim (a.s) faced severe restrictions imposed by these caliphs. The Abbasids were generally hostile to the Shia Imams, viewing them as potential rivals and threats to their rule

Reign of Reign of al-Mansur (r. 754–775)

Abū Jaʿfar ʿAbd Allāh ibn Muḥammad al-Manṣūr, 95 AH – 158 AH/714 CE – 6 October 775 CE usually known simply as by his laqab al-Manṣūr was the second Abbasid caliph, reigning from 136 AH to 158 AH (754 CE – 775 CE) succeeding his brother al-Saffah (r. 750–754). Al-Saffah died after a short five-year reign and al-Mansur took on the responsibility of establishing the Abbasid caliphate by holding on to power for nearly 22 years.

Shia sources blame the Abbasid caliph al-Mansur for the death of Ja'far al-Sadiq, who did not publicly designate an heir, likely fearing the Abbasid reaction. Reports suggest that the caliph ordered his governor of Medina to kill the heir to al-Sadiq, but this plan was thwarted when the governor found that al-Sadiq had appointed four or five legatees. This move created a succession crisis, which was ultimately resolved in favor of Musa al-Kadhim (a.s).

Musa al-Kadhim (a.s) spent the first ten years of his imamate under the rule of al-Mansur. This period was marked by relative calm, possibly because the succession crisis had weakened the mainstream Shia, reducing their immediate threat to the Abbasid regime. Consequently, al-Mansur left al-Kadhim (a.s) relatively unmolested, though he kept him under close surveillance.

However, this initial period of mild treatment did not continue under future caliphs. The following Abbasid rulers, particularly Harun al-Rashid, viewed the Imams and their growing influence with increasing suspicion and hostility. This led to severe restrictions on al-Kadhim (a.s)'s activities and numerous imprisonments throughout his life. Despite these hardships, Imam Musa al-Kadhim (a.s) remained a central figure for his followers, guiding them through a network of representatives and maintaining the spiritual and moral integrity of his community amidst the oppressive Abbasid regime.

Reign of al-Mahdi (r. 775-785)

Abū ʿAbd Allāh Muḥammad ibn ʿAbd Allāh al-Manṣūr (745 – 785), better known by al-Mahdī was the third Abbasid Caliph who reigned from 775 to his death in 785. He succeeded his father, al-Mansur.

During the ten-year reign of Caliph al-Mahdi, Imam Musa al-Kadhim (a.s) remained under close surveillance in Medina. The caliph's suspicion of the Imam's influence led to at least one arrest around 780, resulting in a brief imprisonment in the Abbasid capital of Baghdad. During this imprisonment, al-Kadhim (a.s) was placed in the custody of the prefect of police, al-Musayyab ibn Zuhayr al-Dabbi. Interestingly, al-

Musayyab later became a follower of al-Kadhim (a.s), reflecting the Imam's profound spiritual influence.

The Sunni historian al-Tabari recounts that al-Mahdi had a dream in which Ali ibn Abi Talib, the first Shia Imam and father of al-Kadhim (a.s)'s lineage, berated him for imprisoning his progeny. This dream reportedly compelled al-Mahdi to set Imam Musa al-Kadhim (a.s) free, after extracting a pledge from him not to revolt against the caliphate. This episode highlights the precarious balance the Imams had to maintain: they sought to guide their community spiritually while navigating the dangerous political landscape dominated by the Abbasid caliphs.

Reign of Musa al-Hadi (r. 785–786)

Abū Muḥammad Mūsā ibn al-Mahdī al-Hādī (764 CE – 786 CE) better known by his laqab al-Hādī was the fourth Arab Abbasid caliph who succeeded his father al-Mahdi and ruled from 169 AH (785 CE) until his death in 170 AH (786 CE).

Imam Musa al-Kadhim (a.s) did not lend his support to the 786 revolt of the Alid pretender al-Husayn ibn Ali al-Abid. A letter attributed to al-Kadhim (a.s) even warns al-Husayn about his violent death, demonstrating the Imam's foresight and his caution against armed rebellion. Despite this, the Abbasid caliph al-Hadi accused al-Kadhim (a.s) of complicity in the revolt. The situation became dire, and al-Hadi considered executing the Imam. However, the intervention of the judge Abu Yusuf dissuaded the caliph from this course of action. Shortly thereafter, al-Hadi died suddenly, and Imam Musa al-Kadhim (a.s)'s life was spared.

In gratitude for his survival, Imam Musa al-Kadhim (a.s) composed the supplication Jawshan (lit. 'coat of mail'), according to the Shia jurist Ibn Tawus. This supplication is a testament to the Imam's deep spirituality and his reliance on divine protection in the face of mortal danger. The composition of Jawshan reflects the profound connection between the Imam and his faith, serving as both a personal prayer and a source of spiritual strength for his followers.

Reign of Harun al-Rashid (r. 786–809)

The persecution of the Shia community reached a devastating peak during the caliphate of Harun al-Rashid, who is said to have executed hundreds of Alids, members of the Prophet Muhammad's family through Ali. Harun's hostility extended to Imam Musa al-Kadhim (a.s), whom he arrested and brought to Baghdad. According to some accounts, Harun initially intended to kill al-Kadhim (a.s) but released him following a dream.

Harun's animosity towards al-Kadhim (a.s) may have been exacerbated by an incident recounted by the Sunni historian Ibn Khallikan. During a visit to the tomb of Muhammad in Medina, Harun attempted to assert his familial connection to the Prophet by saying, "Salutation unto thee, O prophet of God, unto thee who art my cousin!" Musa al-Kadhim (a.s), emphasizing his closer lineage, responded with, "Salutation unto thee, O my dear father!" This retort infuriated Harun, who exclaimed, "O Abu al-Hasan [al-Kadhim (a.s)], such glory as thine is truly to be vaunted of!

The final imprisonment of Musa al-Kadhim (a.s) may have been orchestrated by Harun's vizier, Yahya ibn Khalid al-Barmaki. Yahya reportedly felt threatened by the rising influence of Ja'far ibn Muhammad, who was entrusted with the caliph's son and heir, Amin. Yahya allegedly informed Harun of Ja'far's secret Shia inclinations and suborned a relative of al-Kadhim (a.s) to testify that the Imam was covertly collecting religious dues from the Shia.

Alternatively, al-Kadhim (a.s)'s imprisonment might have been due to the caliph feeling threatened by the views of Hisham ibn al-Hakam, a theologian and disciple of al-Kadhim (a.s), who argued for al-Kadhim (a.s)'s right to the caliphate, thereby challenging the legitimacy of the Abbasids. In either case, Harun had al-Kadhim (a.s) arrested in either 793 or 795 and brought to Basra in Iraq. There, al-Kadhim (a.s) was imprisoned for a year under the custody of its governor, Isa ibn Ja'far ibn al-Mansur.

Harun then ordered Isa to kill al-Kadhim (a.s), but Isa, impressed by the Imam's piety, did not comply. Instead, Isa arranged for al-Kadhim (a.s) to be placed under house arrest in Baghdad, initially under Fadl ibn al-Rabi' and later under Fadl ibn Yahya al-Barmaki. Despite the confinement, al-Kadhim (a.s) likely continued to manage Shia affairs

The Abbasid Caliphs, particularly Harun al-Rashid, viewed the Imams as a threat to their political power. Several factors contributed to this perception:

≈ **Legitimacy and Influence:** The Imams, as direct descendants of the Prophet, were seen by many as the rightful leaders of the Muslim community. This posed a challenge to the legitimacy of the Abbasid Caliphs, who had come to power through revolution and political maneuvering rather than hereditary succession.

≈ **Shia Support:** The Shia community, which held the Imams in high esteem, was growing in numbers and influence. This support base could potentially rally against the Abbasid rulers, leading to unrest and rebellion.

≈ **Moral Authority:** The moral and spiritual authority of the Imams was unmatched. Their piety and dedication to Islamic principles contrasted sharply with the often lavish and indulgent lifestyles of the Abbasid court, highlighting the Caliphs' moral shortcomings.

Harun al-Rashid's reign was particularly harsh for Imam Musa al-Kadhim (a.s) and his followers. The Caliph saw the Imam's growing influence as a direct threat and took severe measures to curb it. The persecution took several forms:

≈ **Imprisonment:** Imam Musa al-Kadhim (a.s) spent a significant portion of his life in Abbasid prisons. Harun al-Rashid ordered his arrest multiple times, fearing the Imam's influence and the loyalty he commanded. The Imam was subjected to harsh conditions, isolated from his followers, and moved frequently to prevent any organized support or uprising.

≈ **Surveillance and Harassment**: The Abbasid authorities closely monitored the Imam's activities and those of his followers. Spies were planted to report on their meetings, and anyone found to be in close contact with the Imam risked arrest and punishment.

≈ **Confiscation of Property:** The wealth and properties of the Imam and his followers were often confiscated by the state. This economic pressure was aimed at weakening the financial support base of the Shia community and disrupting their organizational capabilities.

Despite the intense persecution, Imam Musa al-Kadhim (a.s) and his followers remained steadfast in their faith and commitment. They faced numerous struggles:

≈ **Enduring Hardships:** The Imam endured long periods of imprisonment under harsh conditions. His resilience and patience in the face of such adversity became a source of inspiration for his followers.

≈ **Maintaining Secrecy:** The followers of the Imam had to practice their faith and maintain their allegiance in secrecy. They developed covert methods of communication and discreetly supported the Imam's cause, often at great personal risk.

≈ **Upholding Morality:** The followers were often faced with the choice between their safety and their principles. Many chose to uphold the teachings of the Imam, demonstrating immense moral courage and integrity.

When Harun learned of the relatively comfortable conditions under which al-Kadhim (a.s) was living, he sent a written order to Fadl ibn Yahya to execute the Imam. Fadl refused to carry out the order and was subsequently punished with a hundred lashes. Al-Kadhim (a.s) was then transferred to the custody of al-Sindi ibn Shahik, the prefect of police in Baghdad.

It is widely believed that under al-Sindi's supervision, Imam Musa al-Kadhim (a.s) was poisoned, leading to his martyrdom. The Imam's death marked a tragic moment in Shia history, underscoring the intense persecution faced by the Imams and their followers under the Abbasid regime. Despite these trials, the spiritual and moral leadership of Musa al-Kadhim (a.s) left an enduring legacy that continued to inspire and guide the Shia community.

Chapter 5

THE AFTERMATH OF IMAM MUSA AL-KADHIM (a.s)'s MARTYRDOM

The news of Imam Musa al-Kadhim (a.s)'s death sent shockwaves through the Shia community. His martyrdom was not only a profound personal loss but also a significant political and spiritual blow. The community mourned deeply for their beloved Imam, who had guided them through a period of intense persecution with wisdom and piety. His death symbolized the ongoing struggle against the oppressive Abbasid regime and further solidified his followers' resolve to continue his legacy.

The immediate reaction among the Shia was one of grief and outrage. They recognized the martyrdom of their Imam as an act of profound injustice, further fueling their resentment against the Abbasid caliphs. Al-Kadhim (a.s)'s death intensified the sense of martyrdom and persecution that had characterized the Shia identity since the martyrdom of Imam Hussain at Karbala. This collective grief reinforced the Shia community's unity and their commitment to uphold the teachings and principles of their Imams.

One of the most notable reactions came from Bahlol Dana, a well-known figure among the Shia and a contemporary of Imam Musa al-Kadhim (a.s). Bahlol, known for his wisdom and eccentric behavior, had often used his perceived madness to speak truth to power and to protect himself from the caliphs' retribution. His relationship with Imam al-Kadhim (a.s) was one of deep respect and admiration.

Upon hearing the news of the Imam's death, Bahlol's reaction was one of profound sorrow and indignation. He openly mourned the loss of al-Kadhim (a.s), expressing his grief in ways that both comforted and mobilized the Shia community. Through his lamentations and public displays of mourning, Bahlol sought to honor the memory of the Imam and to remind the people of his teachings and sacrifices.

Bahlol's reaction was also characterized by a renewed commitment to resist the injustices of the Abbasid regime. He continued to use his wit and perceived madness to criticize the caliphate and to spread the teachings of the Shia Imams. His actions served to keep the spirit of resistance alive among the Shia, inspiring others to remain steadfast in their faith and principles despite the oppressive political climate.

The death of Imam Musa al-Kadhim (a.s) had significant political and social repercussions. It intensified the existing tensions between the Abbasid caliphs and the Shia community. The martyrdom of al-Kadhim (a.s) was seen as a symbol of the Abbasids' illegitimacy and their brutal tactics to suppress dissent. This further delegitimized the Abbasid rule in the eyes of many and contributed to the growing undercurrent of resistance against their authority.

In the aftermath, the Shia community rallied around Imam Musa al-Kadhim (a.s)'s successor, his son Ali al-Ridha (Imam Ali ar-Ridha). They continued to support and propagate the teachings of their Imams, viewing them as the true spiritual and political leaders of the Muslim ummah. This period also saw the strengthening of the underground network of Shia scholars and representatives, who worked tirelessly to preserve the teachings of their Imams and to organize the community in the face of ongoing persecution.

The memory of Imam Musa al-Kadhim (a.s)'s martyrdom became a powerful narrative within the Shia tradition, symbolizing the enduring struggle for justice, the right to religious freedom, and the importance of standing against tyranny. This narrative not only kept the community united but also inspired future generations to uphold the values and teachings of the Shia Imams.

Let us delve into the captivating journey of Bahlol Dana, the enigmatic figure known as the "wise fool," and explore how his unconventional wisdom transformed the perceptions and ideologies of those around him.

35

Chapter 6

THE LIFE & LEGACY OF BAHLOL DANA

A Mud Palace (Mitti Ka Mahal)

In the opulent palace of Harun al-Rashid, Queen Zubaida gazed out from the magnificent window of her chamber, admiring the breathtaking view of the riverbank. Her eyes caught sight of Bahlol Saheb, seated by the riverside, playing with sand like a child lost in innocent amusement. Intrigued, Zubaida observed his peculiar pastime for a while, then decided to venture out with a few of her attendants to inquire about his curious activity.

Approaching Bahlol Saheb with a mix of curiosity and amusement, Queen Zubaida questioned, "Bahlol Saheb, what are you doing here?"

Bahlol replied with a gleam of mischief in his eyes, "Oh, Your Highness, I am building palaces of paradise."

With this cryptic response, Bahlol resumed his task, engrossed in his imaginative creation. Queen Zubaida

pondered for a moment before asking, "Bahlol Saheb, would you sell these palaces?"

"Certainly, Your Highness, for just two dinars at some texts it is written three dinars, you can own one of these palaces," Bahlol replied casually, his focus undeterred.

Intrigued by his offer, Queen Zubaida promptly handed over two dinars to Bahlol Saheb. With a mischievous grin, Bahlol gestured towards a humble sandcastle nearby, declaring, "Behold, Your Majesty, this palace is now yours."

Queen Zubaida, amused yet puzzled by Bahlol's antics, decided to share the encounter with Emperor Harun. Chuckling at the tale, Harun remarked, "Truly, that madman has bewitched you too, Zubaida! Well, let me rest now."

The next morning, Harun rose with a curious itch to verify the surreal encounter. Venturing out of the palace, he spotted Bahlol Saheb seated by the riverside once again. Approaching him, Harun inquired, "I heard you have begun a trade in selling palaces of paradise, Bahlol Saheb."

Bahlol Saheb, unperturbed, responded, "Indeed, Your Highness, at the cost of half your kingdom."

Harun, taken aback by the audacious demand, exclaimed, "But yesterday, you sold a palace for just two dinars!"

Bahlol Saheb chuckled and retorted, "Your Majesty, Queen Zubaida purchased a palace without seeing it, but you have come to witness these magnificent edifices with your own eyes."

Harun, both amused and astonished by Bahlol's wit, realized the depth of his whimsical wisdom. Though initially bewildered by Bahlol's eccentricity, he now found himself captivated by the profound insights hidden within the facade of madness. Bahlol's playful yet profound perspective challenged Harun's notions of reality, leaving a lasting impression on the emperor's mind.

As Harun reflected on the encounter, he marveled at the enigmatic wisdom of Bahlol Saheb, realizing that sometimes, the most profound truths lie hidden beneath the guise of folly. In the whimsical world of Bahlol Dana, Harun found a mirror reflecting the complexities of human nature and the elusive nature of truth itself.

BAHLOL AND THE BUSSINESSMAN

One day, a prosperous businessman from Baghdad approached Bahlol Dana, seeking his renowned wisdom. With a respectful bow, the businessman addressed him, "Sir Shaykh Bahlol, could you kindly advise me on what I should invest in to gain the most benefit?"

Bahlol, known for his sagacity hidden beneath a veneer of madness, replied thoughtfully, "Invest in iron and cotton."

Taking Bahlol's advice to heart, the businessman went away and invested heavily in iron and cotton. After a few months, the market conditions favored his investments, and he sold his stock for a considerable profit. Delighted with the success, he sought Bahlol out once again.

This time, addressing him with less reverence, the businessman said, "O Crazy Bahlol, what should I buy now to profit me?"

Bahlol, noticing the change in the man's demeanor, responded with a playful glint in his eye, "This time, buy onions and watermelons."

Trusting Bahlol's advice again, the businessman invested his entire savings in onions and watermelons. However, just a few days later, the perishable goods rotted, causing him significant financial loss. In despair and anger, he sought out Bahlol.

"When I first asked you for advice, you told me to buy iron and cotton, and I profited greatly from that. But this time, what kind of advice did you give me? All my wealth has been destroyed!" he exclaimed.

Bahlol, calm and composed, responded, "The first time you addressed me as Shaykh Bahlol, recognizing my wisdom, so I advised you wisely. The second time, you called me Crazy Bahlol, and so I advised you like a crazy person."

The businessman, struck by Bahlol's words, felt a deep sense of shame. He realized his mistake in disrespecting Bahlol and understood the profound lesson in humility and respect that Bahlol had imparted through this experience. From that day forward, the businessman never underestimated the wisdom hidden behind Bahlol's eccentric façade and treated him with the reverence he deserved.

BAHLOL DANA CRITICIZING HARUN AL-RASHID

One day, Bahlol Dana found himself in the presence of Caliph Harun al-Rashid. The caliph, curious about Bahlol's renowned wit and wisdom, decided to engage him in conversation. "O Bahlol!" he called out, "Criticize me, if you dare."

Bahlol, ever ready to impart wisdom through his unique manner, replied, "O Harun, if you found yourself stranded in the desert with no water and you were overcome with severe thirst, near death, what would you give for a single gulp of refreshing water?"

Harun pondered for a moment and answered, "I would give gold dinars."

Bahlol pressed further, "And what if the owner of the water refuses to give it to you for gold dinars? What then would you offer?"

Reflecting on the dire situation, Harun responded, "I would give half of my kingdom."

Bahlol nodded, then continued, "Now, imagine after drinking the water, you fall ill with a condition that prevents you from urinating. What would you give to the one who could cure you of this ailment?"

Harun, seeing where Bahlol's line of questioning was leading, answered, "I would give the remaining half of my kingdom."

With a wise and knowing look, Bahlol concluded, "Then do not place too much value on your kingdom, for it is worth no more than a drink of water. Instead, isn't it proper that you do good with Allah's creations?"

Harun al-Rashid was struck by the profound simplicity of Bahlol's words. He realized the futility of clinging to worldly power and wealth, understanding that true value lies in kindness, compassion, and service to others. Bahlol's criticism, wrapped in a parable, left a lasting impression on the caliph, reminding him of the transient nature of his rule and the importance of virtuous deeds.

46

BAHLOL DANA'S DISCUSSION WITH A FAQIH

It is said that a renowned Faqih (Islamic jurist) from Khorasan arrived in Baghdad. When Caliph Harun al-Rashid heard of this, he invited the Faqih to his court. The jurist was warmly welcomed and seated next to Harun, treated with great respect and honor. During their conversation, Bahlol Dana entered the court. Harun, familiar with Bahlol's wisdom, invited him to take a seat as well.

The Faqih, seeing Bahlol, remarked to Harun, "The Khalifa's favors and preferences are indeed strange, for he honors an ordinary man and seats him close to himself."

Bahlol, understanding the Faqih's scornful comment, turned to him and said, "Do not be arrogant about your so-called knowledge, and do not judge me by my appearance. I am ready to debate with you and prove to the Khalifa that you know nothing."

The Faqih replied dismissively, "I have heard you are insane, and I won't debate with a crazy person."

"I admit my insanity, but you do not acknowledge your ignorance," Bahlol retorted.

Harun Rashid, irritated, ordered Bahlol to be silent, but Bahlol, undeterred, insisted, "If this man is so confident in his knowledge, then he should debate."
Harun turned to the Faqih and said, "What is the difficulty? Ask Bahlol a question."

The Faqih agreed on one condition, "I will ask Bahlol a question. If he answers correctly, I will give him 1,000 dinars. If he cannot answer, he must give me 1,000 dinars."
Bahlol responded, "I have no worldly wealth, not even gold dinars, but I am ready. If I answer your question, I will take the money and distribute it among the poor. If I cannot answer, I will serve you as a servant and slave."

The Faqih agreed and posed his question, "In a house, a wife is sitting with her lawful husband. In that house, one person is praying and another is fasting. Someone from outside enters the house. Because of his arrival, the husband and wife become unlawful for each other, and the prayers and fasts also become unlawful. Can you tell me who the person is?"

Bahlol immediately answered, "The man who entered the house was the woman's first husband, who had gone on a journey. After a long time with no news, it was believed he had died, so the woman, according to Shariah, married the man sitting next to her. She hired two people: one to fulfill her deceased husband's overdue prayers and another to fulfill his missed fasts. When the first husband returned, although he was presumed dead, the other husband became unlawful, as did the prayers and fasts."

Harun and those present praised Bahlol for his accurate and quick resolution of the problem. Bahlol then said, "Now it's my turn to ask a question."

The Faqih agreed, "Ask."

Bahlol asked, "I have one jar of honey and another of vinegar. I want to prepare the refreshing drink Sikanjebeen. I fill one bowl with honey and another with vinegar. When I mix them, I find a mouse in the mixture. Can you tell me if the mouse was in the honey jar or the vinegar jar?"

The Faqih thought for a long time but could not find an answer.

Harun turned to Bahlol and said, "Now, you give the answer."

Bahlol replied, "If this person accepts his lack of knowledge, I will answer the question."

Helpless, the Faqih admitted his ignorance.

Bahlol explained, "We should take the mouse out, wash it with water, and after it is cleaned of honey and vinegar, cut its stomach open. If the stomach contains vinegar, then it fell into the vinegar jar. If it contains honey, it fell into the honey jar."

The entire assembly was astonished by Bahlol's intelligence and knowledge, and they praised him greatly. The Faqih, humbled, bowed his head, and as per the agreement, Bahlol distributed the 1,000 dinars among Baghdad's poor.

HARUN ASKS BAHLOL A QUESTION

One day, Caliph Harun al-Rashid, intoxicated, sat near the river, captivated by the dance of the water waves. In this tranquil moment, Bahlol arrived. Harun, in his drunken state, laughed heartily and warmly welcomed Bahlol, inviting him to sit beside him.

A little while later, Harun turned to Bahlol and said, "Bahlol, today I am going to pose a challenge to you. If you answer correctly, I will reward you with 1,000 dinars. If you fail, I will order you to be thrown from this palace into the river."

Bahlol, ever the wise fool, responded, "I have no need for the dinars, but I will accept your challenge on one condition."

Harun, intrigued, asked, "What is your condition?"

Bahlol replied, "If I answer your question correctly, you must free 100 of my friends who are imprisoned. If I fail, you may throw me into the river."

Harun agreed, and so he posed his riddle, "If I have a goat, a wolf, and a bundle of grass, and I want to ferry them one by one across the river, in what order should I transport them to ensure that the goat doesn't eat the grass and the wolf doesn't eat the goat?"

Bahlol, without missing a beat, answered, "First, take the goat across the river and leave it there. Then return and take the grass across, but leave the grass and bring the goat back with you. Leave the goat on this side and take the wolf across. Leave the wolf with the grass, then return alone to fetch the goat. This way, you can safely transport all three across the river without the goat eating the grass or the wolf eating the goat."

Harun, impressed, exclaimed, "Bravo! You have given the correct answer."

Bahlol then provided the names of his 100 friends, all of whom were loyal followers of the Holy Imam, to be freed. The scribe noted down the names. However, upon receiving and recognizing the names, Harun broke his promise, freeing only ten of Bahlol's friends instead of the agreed hundred.

Though Harun had not fully honored his word, Bahlol's wisdom and courage in the face of such a perilous challenge were clear for all to see, further cementing his legacy as the wise fool who could outwit even the most powerful of rulers.

BAHLOL'S GIFT TO THE KHALIFA

One day, Caliph Harun al-Rashid handed Bahlol some money, instructing him to distribute it among the poor and needy. Bahlol accepted the money but, after a moment of contemplation, handed it back to the Caliph.

Puzzled, Harun asked, "Why did you return the money?"

Bahlol, ever wise and sharp-witted, replied, "I thought long and hard about who might be the most deserving of this charity. In the end, I realized that there is no one more needy and dependent than you, O Caliph. This is why I returned the money."

Harun, taken aback, inquired, "Why do you say I am the most needy?"

Bahlol explained, "I see your guards and officers standing in shops, whipping people, collecting taxes and revenue, and then funneling all these riches into your treasury. Despite all this wealth, your insatiable need for more makes you the most impoverished of all. Thus, I deemed you the most appropriate recipient of your own charity."

Harun was left speechless by Bahlol's insight, realizing the profound truth in his words. This incident not only highlighted Bahlol's wisdom but also served as a powerful reminder of the hollowness of unchecked greed and the true nature of need and wealth.

BAHLOL AND THE THIEF

Bahlol lived in a desolate house across from a cobbler's shop, which had a window facing his home. He used to collect a few dirhams and bury them in the dirt within his house. Whenever he needed money, he would dig up the coins, take what he needed, and bury the rest again.

One day, when Bahlol dug up the dirt to retrieve some coins, he discovered that all his money had disappeared. He immediately suspected that the cobbler, whose window overlooked his house, had stolen the coins.

Without causing any commotion, Bahlol went and sat by the cobbler's shop to chat. Bahlol engaged the cobbler in conversation, slowly earning his trust. When the cobbler seemed at ease, Bahlol said, "Beloved friend, could you keep an account for me?"

The cobbler replied, "Sure, you talk, and I'll keep adding."

Bahlol began talking about various houses and buildings, assigning each a value in coins. Eventually, he mentioned that in his current house, he had buried a certain amount of coins. The cobbler tallied everything up and concluded there was a total of 2,000 dinars.

Bahlol then asked, "O friend, now I need some advice from you."

The cobbler responded, "Of course, speak."

"I want to bury all the coins I have hidden in other places in my current house. What do you think?" Bahlol inquired.

"Very good idea, Bahlol responded, "I have no worldly wealth, not even gold dinars, but I am ready. If I answer your question, I will take the money and distribute it among the poor. If I cannot answer, I will serve you as a servant and slave."

ring all the coins you have hidden and bury them in your present house," the cobbler agreed.

Bahlol pretended to be satisfied and said, "I agree. Now I will go and bring all the coins from other places to bury in that house." Saying this, he left the cobbler.

The cobbler thought to himself, "I will bury those coins I stole back where they were. When Bahlol brings the other coins, I will find them and take all of them at once." He then secretly returned the stolen coins to their original place.

A few hours later, Bahlol returned to his house, examined the area where he kept his money, and saw that the cobbler had indeed reburied the stolen coins. Bahlol retrieved the coins, thanked Allah, and moved to another house.

The cobbler waited a long time for Bahlol to return, but he never did. Eventually, the cobbler realized that Bahlol had outwitted him and reclaimed his money through clever deception.

HARUN QUESTIONS BAHLOL ABOUT HAZRAT ALI

In a moment of sobriety amidst Harun al Rashid's revelry, Bahlol was posed a profound question: was Hazrat Ali ibn Abi Talib greater than the Messenger of Allah's uncle, Abbas' son, or was Abdullah ibn Abbas greater than Ali?

Bahlol, with the weight of truth on his shoulders, fearlessly proclaimed Hazrat Ali's superiority. He painted a portrait of Ali as a paragon of faith, courage, and integrity. Ali's unwavering commitment to Islam, his selflessness on the battlefield, and his devotion to justice were hailed by Bahlol as unmatched virtues.

Bahlol recounted incidents where Ali's actions spoke louder than words, demonstrating his humility and his disdain for personal gain. Even in positions of power, Ali eschewed luxury and upheld principles of fairness and equity. His refusal to tolerate oppression, even among his closest associates, showcased his unwavering commitment to justice.

The story of Ali's confrontation with Ibn Abbas, where Ali demanded accountability for misused public funds, exemplified his commitment to righteousness. Despite familial ties, Ali prioritized justice above all else.

When Harun al Rashid probed about Ali's death, Bahlol recounted the tragic events with solemnity. He described the circumstances of Ali's assassination, According to this account, Abdur Rahman ibn Muljim conspired to kill Hazrat Ali and brought another individual with him. Both perpetrators fell asleep, allowing Hazrat Ali to enter the mosque undetected. As Hazrat Ali performed his prayers, Ibn Muljim launched a cowardly attack, striking Hazrat Ali's head with a poisoned sword.

The blow landed on the same spot where Hazrat Ali had previously been wounded in battle. The poison inflicted a fatal wound, and Hazrat Ali endured three days of suffering before succumbing to his injuries.

In his final moments, Hazrat Ali imparted wise counsel to his sons, emphasizing the superiority of companionship with Allah's friends over worldly attachments. He requested that his murderer, who had inflicted only one blow upon him, be dealt with compassionately, without mutilation.

Hazrat Ali's vision of the Prophet Muhammad, foretelling his imminent reunion, provided solace in his final hours. The celestial signs that accompanied his passing, including changes in the sky's color and the earth's trembling, were interpreted as manifestations of divine presence.

Through this poignant account, the enduring legacy of Hazrat Ali is celebrated, commemorating his unwavering faith, courage, and sacrifice for the sake of Islam.

BAHLOL, A BUNDLE, BARLEY BREAD, AND VINEGAR

This story highlights Bahlol's unconventional wisdom and his unique way of imparting profound lessons. By spending time in the graveyard, Bahlol seeks solace and companionship with those who do not engage in negative behaviors like backbiting and causing harm.

When Harun al asks Bahlol about the events of Qiyamat (the Day of Judgment), Bahlol responds by creating a practical demonstration. He instructs Harun al to have a red-hot iron pan prepared and proposes that they both stand barefoot on it and introduce themselves, describing what they have eaten and worn.

Bahlol swiftly stands on the pan and describes his humble fare of barley bread, vinegar, and tattered clothes. Remarkably, he emerges unscathed from the ordeal. However, when it is Harun al 's turn, he fails to introduce himself in a similar manner and ends up burning his feet, symbolizing the consequences of attachment to worldly splendor.

Through this demonstration, Bahlol conveys the idea that those who lead simple, content lives and are detached from worldly desires will find it easier to pass through the trials of Qiyamat. In contrast, those who are consumed by their attachment to worldly status and wealth will face greater challenges and suffer the consequences of their attachments.

HARUN AND A FRAUD

In the time of Harun al Rashid's reign, a clever fraud devised a scheme to dupe the Khalifa and enrich himself. Posing as an African traveler, he approached Harun al with tales of exotic lands and their treasures. Eager to hear about distant kingdoms and their riches, Harun al engaged the impostor in conversation.

As the conversation progressed, the fraud spun elaborate stories about the harvests, jewels, and inventions of India, captivating Harun al 's imagination. He described a legendary drug purported to restore youth and vitality to those who consumed it, regardless of their age. Intrigued by the promise of such a miraculous elixir, Harun al 's curiosity was piqued.

The fraud, sensing an opportunity to exploit the Khalifa's interest, proposed a deal: he would procure the fabled jewels and the youth-rejuvenating drug in exchange for a hefty sum of 50,000 dinars. Entranced by the descriptions and eager to obtain these marvels, Harun al agreed to the terms and provided the requested payment.

However, as days turned into weeks and weeks into months, there was no sign of the fraudster or the promised treasures. Harun al grew increasingly anxious and regretful, realizing that he had been deceived. His courtiers discussed the matter, expressing their disdain for the impostor's betrayal and speculating about his whereabouts.

It was during this conversation that Bahlol, known for his sharp wit and wisdom, interjected with a tale of his own. Drawing parallels between the Khalifa's predicament and a humorous anecdote involving a rooster, an old woman, and a fox, Bahlol sought to impart a lesson to Harun al .

Tell me whatever the story of the rooster, the old woman, and the fox is, Harun said.

It is said that a wild cat snatched an old woman's rooster. That old woman kept running behind the cat, screaming,

'Come and help me! The cat is taking my one ton- pound rooster!'

"The cat got worried and said, 'O woman! Why did you lie, this rooster isn't as heavy as you said.

"Coincidentally, a fox appeared. It said to the cat, 'Why are you worried and distressed?'

The cat narrated what had occurred.

The fox said, 'Put the rooster on the ground so that I can tell you it's weight.'

As soon as the cat put the rooster on the ground, the fox picked it up, and, while running, said, 'Tell the old woman that my feet say this rooster weighs more than a ton.'

Harun al Rashid laughed a lot at Bahlol's story and praised him.

BAHLOL AND HARUN RASHID GO TO THE PUBLIC BATH

One day, Harun al Rashid, the Khalifa, decided to indulge in the relaxing luxury of a hot bath. Accompanying him was none other than Bahlol, the renowned wise and witty sage, known for his unconventional wisdom and sharp tongue.

As they soaked in the soothing warmth of the bath, the atmosphere was light, and the Khalifa, in a playful mood, decided to engage Bahlol in some banter.

With a mischievous glint in his eye, Harun al Rashid turned to Bahlol and posed a question that carried a hint of jest. "If I were to be considered a slave, Bahlol, what do you suppose would be my price?" he asked, a faint smile playing on his lips.

Bahlol, never one to shy away from a challenge, responded without missing a beat. "Fifty dinars," he declared, his tone calm and matter-of-fact.

The Khalifa, taken aback by Bahlol's audacious response, felt a flicker of indignation rise within him.

"Fifty dinars?" he exclaimed, his voice tinged with incredulity. "Why, that's the price of the lowly skirt I am wearing!"

Unfazed by the Khalifa's reaction, Bahlol maintained his composure, offering a retort that was as

astute as it was daring. "Indeed, Your Majesty," he replied, his voice laced with subtle sarcasm.

"I only assigned the value of the skirt because, as you so rightly pointed out, the Khalifa himself holds no value."

With those words, Bahlol deftly turned the tables on the Khalifa, using humor and wit to subtly underscore a deeper truth.

HARUN QUESTIONS BAHLOL ABOUT WINE

Bahlol's clever analogy about wine, delivered to Harun al Rashid during a moment of revelry, served as a poignant reminder of the dangers of intoxication. Here's how the exchange unfolded:

On a day like any other, Bahlol found himself in the presence of Harun al Rashid, who, indulging in the pleasure of wine, sought to engage the sage in conversation. Seizing the opportunity to impart wisdom, Bahlol listened intently as the Khalifa posed his question.

"Is it forbidden to eat grapes?" Harun al inquired, his tone casual yet curious.

Bahlol, ever the astute thinker, responded without hesitation. "No," he replied simply, knowing well the permissibility of consuming grapes in their natural state.

Encouraged by Bahlol's initial answer, Harun al continued his line of questioning. "What if, after eating grapes, water is drunk over them?" he asked, eager to explore the nuances of Islamic law.

"There is no harm," Bahlol affirmed, his words measured and deliberate.

Seeking further clarification, the Khalifa pressed on. "After eating the grapes and drinking water, one sits for a while in the sun?" he posed, testing Bahlol's knowledge of religious rulings.

"Even then, there is no harm," Bahlol replied calmly, his unwavering confidence evident in his words.

Satisfied with Bahlol's responses thus far, Harun al Rashid, perhaps hoping to make a point, posed a final question. "Then if grapes and water are placed in the sun for a time, how does it become forbidden?" he queried, his voice tinged with curiosity.

Bahlol, ever the master of analogy, seized upon the opportunity to impart a profound lesson. "If some dirt is put on one's head, will it cause any harm?" he asked, redirecting the conversation with finesse.

"No," the Khalifa conceded, recognizing the innocence of such an action.

"Afterwards, if water is poured on it, will it cause any pain?" Bahlol continued, his voice steady and composed.

Again, Harun al Rashid acquiesced. "No," he admitted, acknowledging the benign nature of water on dirt.

Taking a moment to let his words sink in, Bahlol delivered his poignant analogy. "If that dirt and water are mixed to make a brick, and thrown on a person's head, will it cause any pain?" he asked, his voice carrying a weighty significance.

The Khalifa paused, his brow furrowing in contemplation. "True," he finally conceded, understanding the gravity of Bahlol's comparison. "The brick will break a person's head."

With a simple yet profound analogy, Bahlol conveyed a powerful message about the dangers of intoxication. Just as the combination of dirt and water, innocuous on their own, could become a harmful weapon when mixed together, so too could grapes and water, innocent in isolation, become a harmful concoction when transformed into wine. Harun al Rashid, moved by Bahlol's wisdom, ordered the removal of the wine stock, recognizing the importance of heeding the sage's words.

BAHLOL AND THE KEBAB SELLER

This story is my favourite from the life of Bahlol Dana. In the time of Bahlol Dana, a kebab seller was busy preparing kebabs over burning coals. One day, a poor man passed by with a piece of roti that he intended to take home. Seeing the smoke rising from the kebabs, the poor man thought he could warm his roti using the heat from the smoke. He held his roti over the smoke, heated it, and then began to leave.

The kebab seller, noticing this, stopped the poor man and demanded payment. "You used the smoke from my coals to heat your roti, so you owe me money," the seller said angrily.

The poor man, taken aback, protested, "I only used the smoke. Why should I pay for that?"

The kebab seller insisted, "You used my smoke, which came from the coals I used to prepare my kebabs. You must pay for it."

The poor man, now worried, didn't know what to do. Just then, Bahlol happened to pass by. Seeing the distress on the poor man's face, Bahlol approached and asked what the matter was. The poor man explained the situation to Bahlol.

After listening, Bahlol thought for a moment and then said to the poor man, "Give me a dinar."

The poor man, bewildered, replied, "I don't have any money. How can I give you a dinar?"

Bahlol insisted, and reluctantly, the poor man handed him a dinar. Bahlol then turned to the kebab seller and asked, "How much does this man owe you?"

"Three dirhams," the seller responded.

Bahlol took the dinar and tossed it three times, producing a sound each time it hit the ground. The seller, confused, asked, "What are you doing?"

Bahlol smiled and replied, "The man used the smoke from your coals, and now you have heard the sound of the coins. You got what you deserved—sound for smoke."

The people standing around were astonished by Bahlol's cleverness. The kebab seller, realizing the fairness in Bahlol's judgment, had nothing more to say. The poor man thanked Bahlol profusely for his wisdom and intervention.

BAHLOL CRITICIZES

One day, Abdullah Mubarak ventured into the desert to seek the wisdom of Bahlol the Wise. As he approached, he found Bahlol bareheaded and barefoot, engrossed in reciting Allah's Name. Abdullah greeted him with a salute, which Bahlol acknowledged.

"O Shaykh!" Abdullah began. "My request is that you advise me on how to live in this world so that I stay away from sins. I am a sinful being and can't overcome my evil self-will. Tell me some way by which I can find relief."

Bahlol responded, "O Abdullah! I myself am worried and distressed. What do you expect from me? If I had a brain, people wouldn't call me crazy. What effect can the speeches of lunatics have that people would accept? So, go and look for some intelligent person."

But Abdullah persisted. "O Shaykh! Those who say they are crazy are just fooling others. They are intelligent, and it is the truth that is heard from the lunatic."

Bahlol was silent for a moment, then Abdullah continued to flatter him, "O Shaykh! Don't disappoint me; I came with expectations."

"O Abdullah!" Bahlol finally replied. "First agree to my four conditions, so that you don't go back on your words at the statement of a lunatic. Then I will criticize you and will tell you such things that will be the means of your salvation."

"What are these four conditions?" Abdullah asked. "Tell me so I can agree."

"Firstly, whenever you commit a sin or go against Allah's command, do not eat of His sustenance."

"Then whose sustenance shall I eat of?" Abdullah queried.

"Being an intelligent person, you claim that you worship Allah and eat of His sustenance, and then you disobey His command. You yourself judge, is this the way to repay beneficence?"

Abdullah admitted, "You spoke true. What is the second condition?"

"Secondly, whenever you want to sin, do not intend to stay in His Kingdom."

"This is more difficult than the first because every place is Allah's land and kingdom. Where will I go?"

"It is a very evil thing that you eat of His sustenance, live in His Kingdom, and then disobey His command. Judge for yourself, is this the condition of beneficence?"

"What is the third condition?" Abdullah asked.

"Thirdly, when you want to sin or disobey His command, then go hide in such a place where He can't see or be aware of you. Then do whatever you want."

"This is the most difficult," Abdullah admitted. "Allah knows and sees all. He is present everywhere. He sees and knows all that His creations do."

"You are an intelligent being. You should know that He is present everywhere, the All-Knowing and All-Seeing. In this sense, it would be very evil of you to eat of His sustenance, stay in His Kingdom, and then disobey Him in His All-Knowing, All-Seeing presence. Even then, you claim to worship Him; although He says in the Holy Qur'an, 'Do not think that Allah is unaware of the act of the oppressor.'"

"You spoke true. What is the fourth condition?" Abdullah asked.

"The fourth condition is that when the Angel of Death suddenly comes to you to obey Allah's order and seize your soul, then at that time say, 'Wait a little while so I can say goodbye to my relatives, get their farewell, and take provisions for my last journey; then seize my soul.'"

"This is the most difficult condition," Abdullah confessed. "At that time, the Angel of Death will not even give me time to breathe."

"O intelligent human! You know that there is no cure for death. You can't make it go away from you, and the Angel of Death doesn't give time when on the verge of death. While committing sins, the Angel of Death suddenly and surprisingly comes, sparing no time for even breathing. As Allah says, 'When the time of their death comes, they can't hurry a bit or delay.' So then, Abdullah! Hear the truth from a lunatic and awaken from the sleep of unawareness."

"Beware of arrogance and intoxication, and worry about the Hereafter because a long journey waits and life is short. Don't postpone today's work until tomorrow; maybe tomorrow will not come for you. Know that this is the most valuable time. Don't be lazy in doing work for the Hereafter. Make provision for the Hereafter today because regretting there tomorrow has no benefit."

When Abdullah heard these words, he bowed his head and began to think. Bahlol again spoke, "O Abdullah! You wanted advice from me that would prove useful tomorrow and wanted me to present an example and proof. Why have you bowed your head? What answer will you give on the Day of Judgment when dangerous and strong angels inquire during your reckoning? Today, whomever's account is pure will have no fear tomorrow."

Finally, Abdullah raised his head and said, "O Shaykh! I wholeheartedly listened to your advice. I also accept this fourth condition. Say something else and make me your student."

"O Abdullah! It is incumbent upon the servant that whatever he does is by Allah's order and whatever he says or hears is according to His order; then the servant is a servant."

The wise Bahlol, known as a lunatic by many, had indeed benefitted from the companionship of Imam Jafar Sadiq.

FAZL BIN RABI BUILDS A MOSQUE

Fazl bin Rabi', a prominent and influential official during the reign of Harun al-Rashid, decided to construct a mosque in Baghdad. Upon its completion, the people suggested placing a plaque on its door to commemorate its construction. Fazl was approached for his opinion on what should be inscribed on the plaque. Bahlol, known for his wisdom and unconventional approach to matters, was also present during this discussion.

Bahlol asked Fazl, "Who did you build the mosque for?"

Fazl replied, "For Allah."

Bahlol then said, "If you made it for Allah, then don't inscribe your name on the plaque."

Fazl, taken aback and slightly irritated, responded, "Why shouldn't I have my name inscribed on the tablet? People have to know who the maker of the mosque is!"

Bahlol suggested, "Then have it inscribed that the maker of this mosque is Bahlol."

Fazl, becoming angrier, retorted, "I certainly will not have that written!"

Bahlol calmly explained, "If you made this mosque for fame and self-show, then you have lost your reward."

Fazl speechless and reflective, realized the truth in Bahlol's words. The wisdom in Bahlol's argument struck a chord with him, and he acknowledged that seeking fame would nullify the sincerity of his act of building the mosque for Allah's sake.

Finally, Fazl conceded, "Whatever Bahlol says, have that inscribed."

Bahlol, seeing the change in Fazl's attitude, said, "Have a verse from the Sacred Qur'an inscribed on the door of the mosque."

Thus, a verse from the Qur'an was inscribed on the mosque's door, signifying the true intention behind the construction—a sincere act dedicated to Allah, devoid of personal vanity and pride. This story not only reflects Bahlol's wisdom but also serves as a timeless reminder of the importance of sincerity in acts of worship and charity.

HARUN AL RASHID'S ANGER AND BAHLOL'S FORGIVENESS

One day, Harun al Rashid, the Abbasid Caliph, grew suspicious of Bahlol's loyalty and decided to investigate his faith and allegiance. Harun al hired a spy to find out more about Bahlol's religious beliefs and political inclinations. After a few days, the spy returned with his report, revealing that Bahlol was a devoted friend of the Ahlul Bayt and a faithful follower of Musa bin Jafar.(a.s)

Harun al , angered by this information, summoned Bahlol and confronted him. "I have heard that you are among the friends and lovers of Musa bin Jafar and that you propagate his rights against me. To save yourself from punishment, you have pretended to be insane."

Bahlol responded calmly, "If that is so, then how will you treat me?"

Harun al 's anger flared even more at Bahlol's composed demeanor. In a fit of rage, he commanded his slave Masroor, "Take Bahlol's clothes off and put a donkey's saddle on his back. Put the donkey's rein in his mouth, then parade him around the palace and its surroundings. After that, cut off his head in front of me."

Masroor followed Harun al 's orders. He stripped Bahlol of his clothes, saddled him like a donkey, and led him around the palace grounds. After the humiliating parade, Masroor presented Bahlol to Harun al , ready to execute the final order.

At that moment, Jafar Barmaki, a high-ranking official and advisor, happened to be present. Seeing Bahlol in such a degrading state, Jafar asked, "Bahlol! What was your mistake?"

Bahlol, ever quick-witted, replied, "Since I told the truth, the Khalifa gave me his own garments as a reward."

This response elicited laughter from Harun al , Jafar, and everyone else present. Harun al 's anger dissipated, and he decided to forgive Bahlol. He ordered

Masroor to remove the saddle and reins and to bring new, fine clothes for Bahlol.

However, Bahlol refused to accept the new clothes. He picked up his old, tattered garments and left the palace, once again demonstrating his wisdom and humility.

This story showcases Bahlol's cleverness and the power of truth, even in the face of severe punishment. It also highlights the capricious nature of Harun al Rashid, whose anger turned to laughter and forgiveness due to Bahlol's witty remark.

HARUN RASHID AND A HUNTER

One Eid day, Harun al Rashid, the Abbasid Caliph, was playing chess with his wife Zubaydah. Bahlol, known for his wisdom and wit, approached and sat nearby to observe. A hunter entered, kissed the floor in greeting, and presented Harun al with a splendid, fat fish as a gift. Harun al , intoxicated at the time, impulsively ordered that the hunter be rewarded with 4,000 dirhams.

Zubaydah, concerned about the extravagant reward, admonished Harun al , "This amount is too much for the hunter. If you give such large rewards every day in the forts and cities, others will feel undervalued compared to a mere hunter, and if you give them more, the treasury will soon be empty."

Harun al , recognizing the wisdom in her words, asked, "What should I do then?"

Zubaydah suggested, "Call the hunter back and ask if the fish is male or female. If he says it is female, say you don't like it; if he says it is male, also say you don't like it. He will have no choice but to leave without his reward."

Bahlol, sensing the unfairness, advised Harun al , "Do not be swayed by a woman's advice. Do not dishearten the hunter."

However, Harun al ignored Bahlol's counsel and summoned the hunter, asking, "Is this fish male or female?"

The hunter, quick-witted, replied, "This fish is neither male nor female; it is actually an eunuch."

Pleased with the clever answer, Harun al ordered that the hunter be given another 4,000 dirhams. The hunter gratefully accepted the reward and left. As he descended the palace stairs, a dirham fell to the ground. The hunter bent down and picked it up. Zubaydah, observing this, remarked to Harun al , "What a lowly person, he cannot even part with a single dirham."

Harun al , agreeing with Zubaydah, called the hunter back. Again, Bahlol cautioned, "Do not call him back."

Ignoring Bahlol, Harun al confronted the hunter, "How base must you be to not even leave one dirham for the slaves when you have received so much?"

The hunter respectfully replied, "I am not base, but I know the value of grace. I picked up the dirham because it bears a Quranic verse on one side and the Caliph's honorable name on the other. Leaving it on the ground would lead to disrespect if it were stepped on."

Harun al , impressed once more, ordered an additional 4,000 dirhams be given to the hunter. Bahlol remarked, "Didn't I advise you not to stop him?"

Harun, realizing his mistake, admitted, "I am crazier than you, Bahlol. You warned me three times, yet I did not heed your advice. By following Zubaydah's suggestion, I have incurred this loss."

This story highlights Bahlol's wisdom, the importance of fairness, and the unintended consequences of not listening to good advice. Harun al 's actions, driven by pride and impulsiveness, contrasted with Bahlol's consistent advocacy for just treatment and consideration.

HARUN AL RASHID'S QUESTION ABOUT AMEEN AND MAMOON

One day, as Bahlol was heading towards Harun al 's palace, he coincidentally encountered the Caliph. Harun al inquired about Bahlol's destination, to which Bahlol replied that he was on his way to see Harun al . Surprised, Harun al invited Bahlol to accompany him to the school, expressing his desire to closely observe Ameen and Mamoon.

Upon arriving at the school, they discovered that Ameen and Mamoon had stepped out with the teacher's permission. Harun al , keen to know more about them, asked the teacher for insights into their characters. The teacher described Ameen as foolish and stupid, despite being the son of Zubaydah, the esteemed Arab woman. In contrast, Mamoon was portrayed as intelligent, understanding, and dignified.

Harun al expressed skepticism, prompting the teacher to devise a test. He placed a piece of paper under Mamoon's seat and a brick under Ameen's. Upon their return, Mamoon nervously observed that the floor seemed higher or the ceiling lower since his departure, deducing that his seat was now slightly elevated. In contrast, Ameen felt no such difference.

Impressed by the demonstration, Harun al asked Bahlol for an explanation. Bahlol, however, hesitated, seeking assurance for his life before revealing the reason. Harun al obliged, and Bahlol began to expound.

He elucidated that intelligence in children often stems from two factors: the love and compatibility between the parents and the diversity of their bloodlines. Bahlol likened it to the grafting of fruit trees or the breeding of animals. When individuals from different backgrounds unite, their offspring often inherit traits of intelligence and vitality.

Bahlol then humorously pointed out that Ameen's lack of understanding was due to the close blood relation between Harun al and Zubaydah. In contrast, Mamoon's brilliance stemmed from his mother's lineage, which differed significantly from Harun al 's.

Though Harun al rashid laughed off Bahlol's explanation as the musings of a lunatic, the teacher was convinced of its validity, acknowledging the wisdom in Bahlol's words.

BAHLOL'S CONVERSATION WITH ABU HANIFA

One day, Abu Hanifa was teaching at his college, with Bahlol seated quietly in a corner, listening to the lesson. During his lecture, Abu Hanifa challenged three teachings of Imam Jafar Sadiq, stating his disagreements:

1. Imam Jafar Sadiq claimed that Shaitan would be punished in Hell-fire. Abu Hanifa argued that since Shaitan is made of fire, fire cannot hurt him. One kind of substance cannot harm the same kind of substance.

2. Imam Jafar Sadiq taught that Allah cannot be seen, but Abu Hanifa believed that anything present must be visible to the eyes.

3. Imam Jafar Sadiq asserted that individuals are responsible for their own actions and will be questioned for them, but Abu Hanifa countered that all actions are determined by Allah, leaving individuals without control.

As soon as Abu Hanifa made these statements, Bahlol picked up a clod of earth and threw it at Abu Hanifa,

hitting his forehead and causing him severe pain. Bahlol then fled the scene. Abu Hanifa's students chased after him, eventually capturing him and bringing him before the Khalifa, recounting the incident.

When Bahlol was brought before the Khalifa, he requested that Abu Hanifa be summoned to present his response. Once Abu Hanifa arrived, Bahlol asked, "What wrong have I done to you?"

Abu Hanifa, nursing his pain, replied, "You hit my forehead with a clod of earth. My forehead and head are in severe pain."

Bahlol then asked, "Can you show me your pain?"

Perplexed, Abu Hanifa responded, "Can pain be seen?"

Bahlol seized the moment and said, "You yourself claim that everything present can be seen, yet you now admit that pain, which is present, cannot be seen. Secondly, you stated that a clod of earth, being made of mud, cannot hurt you since humans are also made of mud. If your logic were true, how could the clod of earth cause you pain? Lastly, you argued that all actions are performed by Allah, not by individuals. If that is the case, how can you accuse me, present me to the Khalifa, and seek punishment for my actions?"

Abu Hanifa, realizing the wisdom in Bahlol's arguments, left the court of Harun al Rashid in shame and embarrassment.

Chapter 7

THE ENDURING LEGACY OF BAHLOL DANA

The life of Bahlol Dana, often cloaked in the guise of madness, has left an indelible mark on the annals of Islamic history and literature. His seemingly eccentric behavior and insightful wisdom continue to resonate, offering timeless lessons that transcend the ages.

The tales are not merely stories of a bygone era; they are repositories of moral and ethical teachings. His interactions with Harun al Rashid, the esteemed scholars of his time, and ordinary people showcase his unique ability to blend humor with profound insight. Through his unconventional methods, Bahlol was able to critique power, question societal norms, and uphold justice in ways that were accessible and memorable to all. Bahlol Dana's love and loyalty to the Ahlul Bayt, especially to

Imam Musa al-Kadhim(a.s), exemplify his deep commitment to the teachings of the Prophet Muhammad and his family. In an era where expressing support for the Imams often led to persecution and death, Bahlol's open allegiance was a testament to his courage and steadfastness. His life is a shining example of how true justice and fidelity to the Messenger of Allah and his progeny are paramount, even at the cost of personal safety and comfort. One of the most compelling aspects of Bahlol's legacy is his unwavering humility and piety. Despite having access to the highest echelons of power, he chose a life of asceticism and simplicity. His actions and words were deeply rooted in the teachings of Islam, emphasizing the transient nature of worldly possessions and the eternal value of righteousness. Bahlol Dana, also known as Bahlol the Wise, is believed to be buried in the Kadhim (a.s)ayn area of Baghdad, Iraq. His tomb is located in the vicinity of the Al-Kadhim (a.s)ayn Shrine, which is a significant site for Shia Muslims, as it also houses the graves of the seventh and ninth Shia Imams, Musa al-Kadhim (a.s) and Muhammad al-Jawad.

The exact location of Bahlol's grave within this area is not clearly marked or widely recognized, but the general belief is that he rests somewhere near these important religious figures.

The Kadhimayn (a.s) area is a place of pilgrimage for many Shia Muslims, who visit to pay their respects to the Imams and, by extension, to other notable figures like Bahlol Dana.

Upon his death, the people of Baghdad mourned the loss of their beloved wise fool, recognizing the depth of his knowledge and the value of his lessons, which often came disguised in madness. His legacy lived on through the many stories and anecdotes that highlighted his cleverness, wisdom, and the moral teachings he imparted.

There isn't a specific, widely accepted historical record detailing the exact circumstances of Bahlol's death, and much of what is known comes from the oral traditions and folklore that celebrate his life and wisdom.

Bahlol Dana's stories have been passed down through generations, becoming an integral part of Islamic folklore and education. His life is a subject of study and admiration, embodying the virtues that Islam espouses. Through his wit and wisdom, Bahlol Dana has earned a place not just in history, but in the hearts and minds of those who seek guidance and inspiration.

AUTHOR'S NOTE

Since childhood, I have been captivated by the stories of Bahlol Dana. My grandmother would often recite his tales, weaving them into the fabric of my upbringing. As I listened to the exploits of this enigmatic figure, I found myself deeply inspired by his life and the way he chose to navigate the world.

Bahlol's unwavering commitment to truth, justice, and humility left an indelible mark on my imagination. His courage in the face of adversity, his wit in the face of power, and his compassion in the face of cruelty continue to resonate with me to this day.

It is this admiration and fascination that led me to embark on the journey of writing this book. I wanted to delve deeper into the life of Bahlol, to uncover the layers of wisdom hidden within his seemingly foolish antics, and to share his remarkable story with a wider audience.

I am grateful to you, dear reader, for opening the pages of this book and delving into the life of the wise fool of Baghdad. It is my sincere hope that these pages have brought a smile to your face, sparked a thought in your mind, and perhaps even stirred a longing for the timeless wisdom of Bahlol Dana.

Thank you for joining me on this journey.

Warm regards,

Mohd Asad Naqvi